GW00724761

Published by

Lonely Planet Publications Pty Ltd
A.B.N. 36 005 607 983
90 Maribyrnong St, Footscray,
Victoria, 3011, Australia

Lonely Planet Offices

Australia
Locked Bag 1, Footscray, Victoria, 3011

USA
150 Linden Street, Oakland, CA 94607

UK
72-82 Rosebery Avenue, London, EC1R 4RW, UK

Printed through Colorcraft Ltd, Hong Kong

Printed in China

Text and maps © Lonely Planet 2006

Images © Lonely Planet Images, except those marked *, © Getty Images

ISBN 1 74059 890 3

Travel Journal

the journey begins

personal information

name

address

phone

email

important numbers

passport no.   driving licence no.

travel insurance no.   camera serial no.

other

medical information

blood group   doctor

allergies / medication

emergency contact

other

if found, please return to

travel schedule

journey

date   flight   ticket

depart   arrive

journey

date   flight   ticket

depart   arrive

journey

date   flight   ticket

depart   arrive

journey

date   flight   ticket

depart   arrive

journey

date   flight   ticket

depart   arrive

journey

date   flight   ticket

depart   arrive

journey

date | flight | ticket

depart | arrive

journey

date | flight | ticket

depart | arrive

journey

date | flight | ticket

depart | arrive

journey

date | flight | ticket

depart | arrive

journey

date | flight | ticket

depart | arrive

journey

date | flight | ticket

depart | arrive

travel schedule

journey _____

date _____ flight _____ ticket _____

depart _____ arrive _____

journey _____

date _____ flight _____ ticket _____

depart _____ arrive _____

journey _____

date _____ flight _____ ticket _____

depart _____ arrive _____

journey _____

date _____ flight _____ ticket _____

depart _____ arrive _____

journey _____

date _____ flight _____ ticket _____

depart _____ arrive _____

journey _____

date _____ flight _____ ticket _____

depart _____ arrive _____

journey _____

date _____ flight _____ ticket _____

depart _____ arrive _____

journey _____

date _____ flight _____ ticket _____

depart _____ arrive _____

journey _____

date _____ flight _____ ticket _____

depart _____ arrive _____

journey _____

date _____ flight _____ ticket _____

depart _____ arrive _____

journey _____

date _____ flight _____ ticket _____

depart _____ arrive _____

journey _____

date _____ flight _____ ticket _____

depart _____ arrive _____

addresses

name

address

telephone

email

name

address

telephone

email

name

address

telephone

email

name

address

telephone

email

name

address

telephone

email

name

address

telephone

email

name

address

telephone

email

name

address

telephone

email

name

address

telephone

email

name

address

telephone

email

addresses

name

address

telephone

email

name

address

telephone

email

name

address

telephone

email

name

address

telephone

email

name

address

telephone

email

name

address

telephone

email

name

address

telephone

email

name

address

telephone

email

name

address

telephone

email

name

address

telephone

email

addresses

name

address

telephone

email

name

address

telephone

email

name

address

telephone

email

name

address

telephone

email

name

address

telephone

email

name

address

telephone

email

name

address

telephone

email

name

address

telephone

email

name

address

telephone

email

name

address

telephone

email

Kabul, Afghanistan

PAULA BRONSTEIN

RAJASTHAN, INDIA

Rajasthan, the Land of the Kings, is India's most colour-charged state. Half desert, half bony hills, the everyday is shot with searing colour – brilliant fabrics flash like flames against the stark landscape. You'll experience these saturated shocks of colour everywhere – a sea of turbans clustered under a village tree, rural women in traditional dress, saris drying on a parched riverbed. Like a legend come to life, the state is packed with magical towns and cities: sky-blue Jodhpur; Jaipur, painted dusky pink; Jaisalmer, a golden sandcastle; Udaipur, shimmering bone-white; and Pushkar, clinging around its holy lake. And let's not forget the state's unparalleled contributions to the art of the moustache: tradition dictates this should be groomed, thick, kinkily curved and stiffly gesturing skywards.

Ushuaia, Argentina

MICHAEL COYNE

SHANGHAI, CHINA

Whore of the Orient, Paris of the East; city of quick riches, ill-gotten gains and fortunes lost on the tumble of dice; the domain of socialites and swindlers, adventurers and drug runners, tycoons, missionaries, gangsters and pimps – Shanghai has a history so impregnated with myth that it's hard to decide whether it was once a paradise or an all-encompassing evil. The city put away its dancing shoes in the Mao years, when the masses shuffled instead to the dour strains of Marxist-Leninism and the wail of the factory siren. But today, Shanghai is once again a sucker for showiness, and it's this trait that fires the economy and supplies the city with its hi-octane verve.

Vienna, Austria

MARTIN GENT

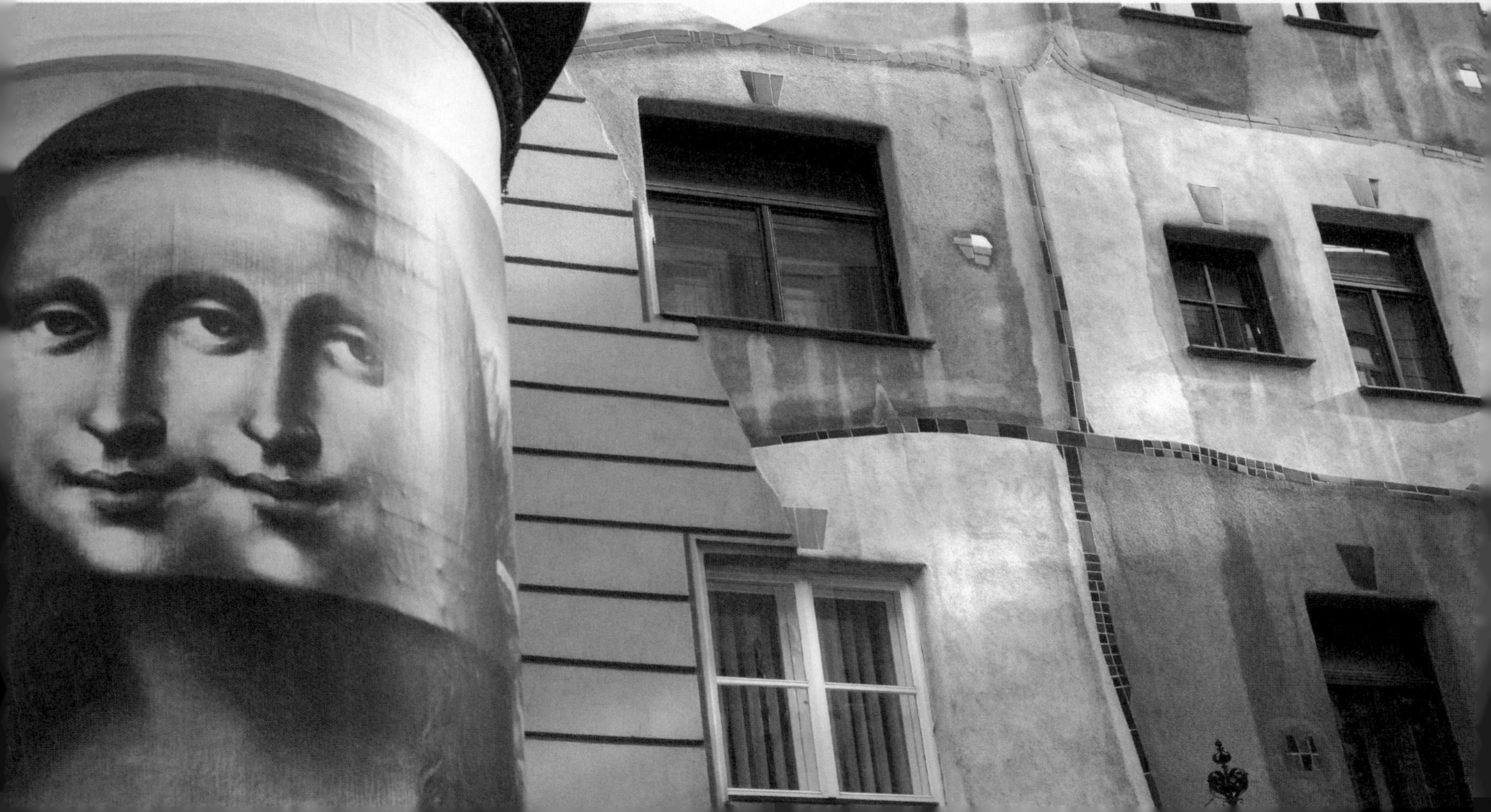

LAS VEGAS, USA

A surreal apparition rising out of barren desert sands, at first glance Las Vegas appears a shimmering mirage, a figment of your imagination. An otherworldly, schizophrenic, bold and blazing creation of some demented cartoon artist. An alternate universe, where the globe's most famous sights – ancient Egypt's pyramids, Paris' Eiffel Tower, the canals of Venice – tumble together, bathed in an ethereal neon glow. Fused by greed, driven by lust, pulsating with passion, Las Vegas embodies the shady side of the American Dream. It's a place where inhibitions are temporarily lost, sins forgotten and fate decided by the spin of a roulette wheel.

PERU

If Peru didn't exist, travel guide books would have to invent it. It's a land of lost cities and ancient ruins, brooding Andean peaks and trashy urban beaches. It's dense jungles and overcrowded cities, mysterious Incan rites and Roman Catholic masses, practising shamans and dashboard Virgin Marys, Shining Path guerrillas and ex-shoeshine-boys for president. And where hats are funky and there's a weird affection for the last scene from *Dirty Dancing*. It's like the whole world in a snow dome.

Belize City, Belize

ANTHONY PLUMMER

CANADA

The Creator must have been in an especially good mood when designing Canada. There are big-shouldered mountains chiselled into rugged splendour by glaciers and the elements. Across the prairies, fields of golden wheat wave gently in the wind, sheltered by a cerulean sky. The cry of the loon and the howl of the wolf drift over vast expanses of wilderness where nature still grandstands, raw, pristine and fierce. Pathways off the beaten track lead you to grazing moose and burly bears, while the skies are darkened by gargantuan skeins of Canada geese. Rainforests, serpentine coastlines, a gazillion streams, the eternal blanket of arctic ice and even a small desert – all are parts of the vast and unique natural patchwork that is Canada.

ОТКРИВАНЕ 31 АВГУСТ

Sofia, Bulgaria

КОЛ

DOUG McKINLAY

MADAGASCAR

The first Europeans
to reach Madagascar
returned home with
stories of baboons 7ft
tall and man-eating
trees. On reflection,
these seem to be the
only two species the
island hasn't laid
claim to at some
point in its ecological
history. The island
has evolved a teeming
mass of animals and
plants unknown
anywhere else on
earth: jumping rats,
hissing cockroaches,
moths as big as
dinner plates and
chameleons the size
of matchsticks, not to
mention something
that looks like a teddy
bear and sounds like
a police car. Not that
Madagascar's human
inhabitants are exactly
dull either. Rites of
honour to the dead,
sacred waterfalls,
spirit caves and a
complex web of beliefs
and taboos bind them
powerfully to the
natural world and
the ancestors they
venerate.

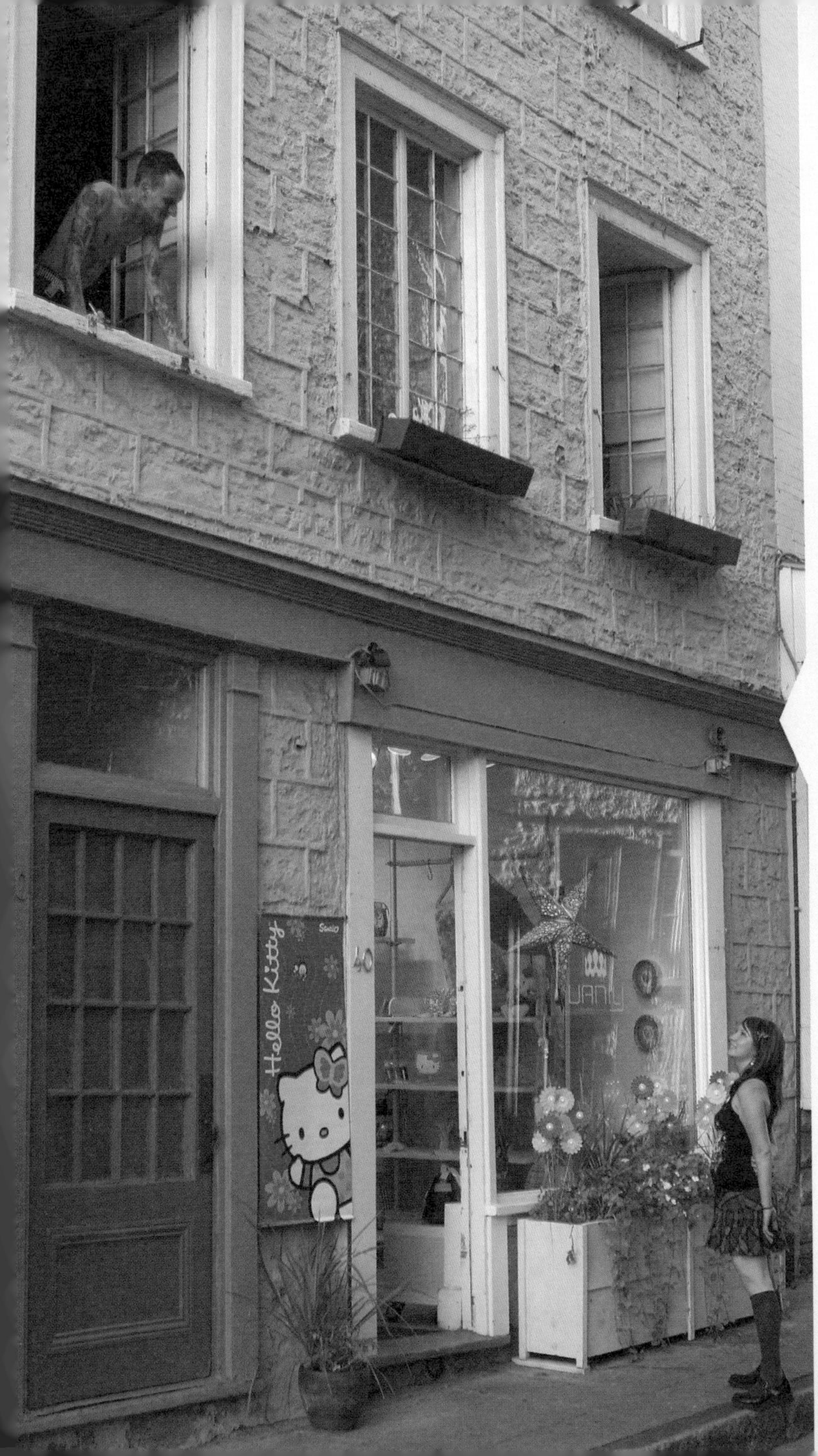

Montréal, Canada

CHRIS CHEADLE

DATE ◯◯◯

KYRGYZSTAN

What Kyrgyzstan lacks in gracious buildings and fancy cakes, it makes up for with nomadic traditions such as laid-back hospitality, a healthy distrust of authority and a fondness for drinking fermented mare's milk. For decades, even centuries, this place has been out of focus, a blank on the map of empires. Even today, to those not in the know, 'Central Asia' brings to mind a desert wasteland of illiterate nomads. The reality, in this addictive and fascinating part of the world, is that nothing could be further from the truth.

Cartagena, Colombia

PATRICIA RINCON MAUTNER

ARGENTINA

Throughout Latin America and much of the world, Argentines endure a reputation for being snobbish European wannabes who regard themselves as superior to other Latin Americans. They think that they're economically superior (they once were), that they play the best soccer (they often do), that they have the most beautiful women (depends on your taste), and that they dance the most sophisticated dance in the world (no contest). Indeed, the classic Argentine stereotype is grounded, at least partially, in truth. But anyone who spends some time in Argentina finds the stereotype immediately challenged by warmth, friendliness and the gregarious social nature that more accurately defines the Argentine psyche.

GREENLAND

Greenland's rugged and dramatic landscape can be forbidding at times, and the country's diversity is expressed in subtle variations on Arctic conditions: rocky, treeless mountains; dry or boggy tundra; long, sinuous fjords; and expansive sheets and tortured rivers of ice. Much of coastal Greenland meets the sea in towering cliffs, walls of glacial ice and ancient rock – the oldest on the planet. The seas, near which all the population is found, are just a couple of degrees above freezing, and are infested with mountains of floating ice.

OPERA DELLA METROPOLITANA

SENEGAL

Senegal is an all-singing, all-dancing extravaganza with a contagious and constantly restless beat. The capital Dakar is the kind of city that activates the adrenal glands, while in contrast St-Louis is a kind of elegant old colonial lady who dreams of long-ago aviation heroes in safari suits. The endless golden beaches can be enjoyed from sleepy fishing villages or plush Western-style resort towns, and the national parks rank among the region's best. Down south, Casamance is like a troubled movie starlet, desired and pitied by everyone. Wherever you go, the Senegalese people constantly amuse and occasionally exasperate with their boundless wit, smooth-talking charm and irrepressible will to connect.

MES JAU DIRBAME

SYDNEY, AUSTRALIA

Sydney is that rare example of good things coming together in harmony. Its location is superb – long stretches of heavenly beaches and waterfront; a pleasant climate that encourages people to get out and about; and a population of open-minded, outgoing entrepreneurial types who are itching to show the whole place off. Sydney has its knockers, but they tend to be people who haven't lived there, loved there and laughed there – or who are easily intimidated by the 'brash flash trash' façade. After all, it's not as if bouncers are posted at Sydney's door, sussing out the crowd and only letting the beautiful people in – it just looks that way when the umpteenth über-spunk glides by on rollerblades or in a convertible.

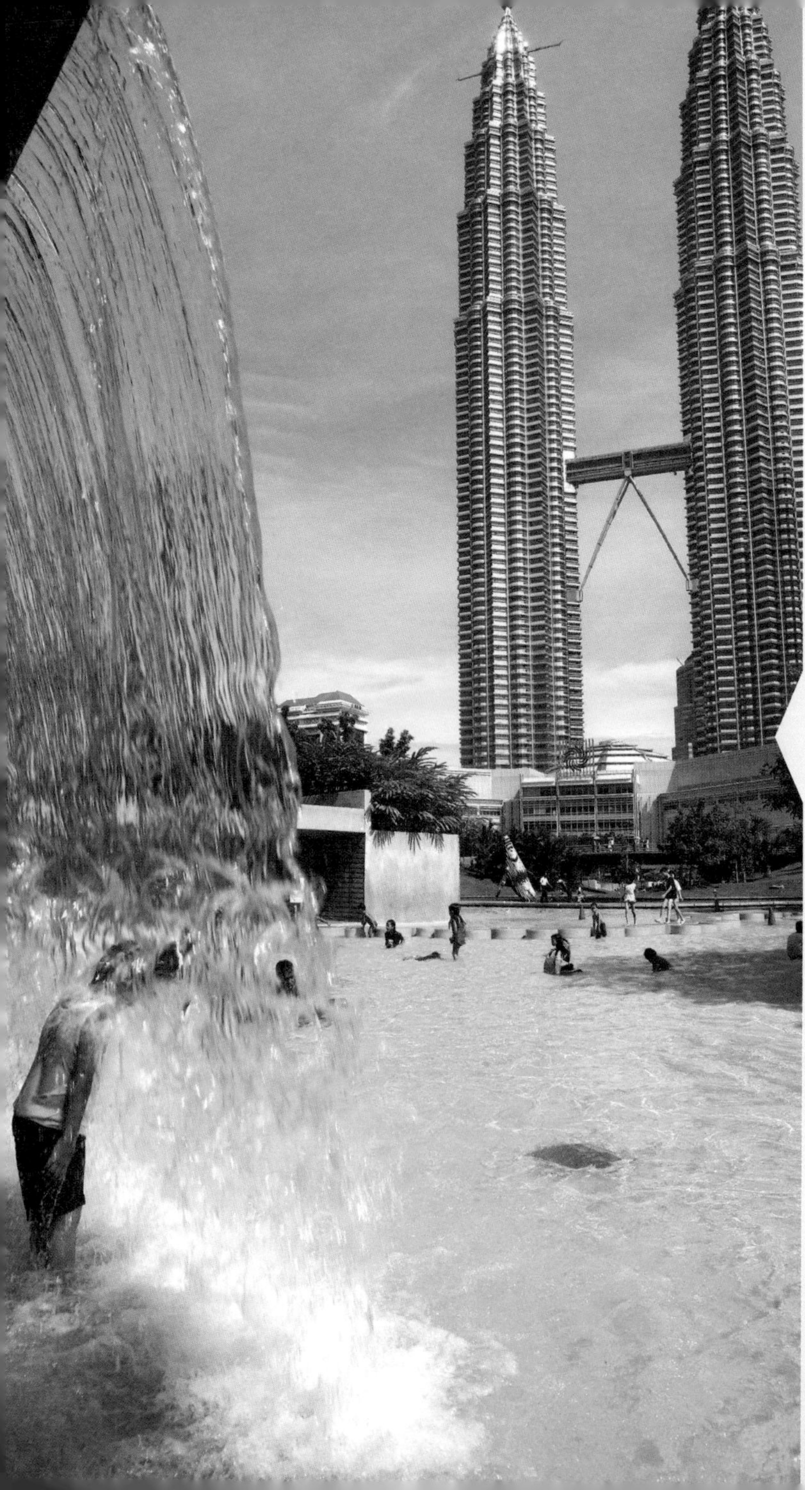

Kuala Lumpur, Malaysia

GREG ELMS

CUBA

You've heard about the socialism and salsa. You know that the cigars are world class and the cars are classic. But what no travelogue or movie can convey are the all-night rumbas (now that's dirty dancing!), the drum-induced trance of a Santería ceremony, the reggae jams on the banks of the Río Almendares, the deserted beaches, the secret waterfalls or the teeming coral reefs. While Fidel's infrastructure has seen better decades and the food is, well, best not spoken about, the last great bastion of communism challenges and enchants with its intoxicating human spirit. Or was that the rum?

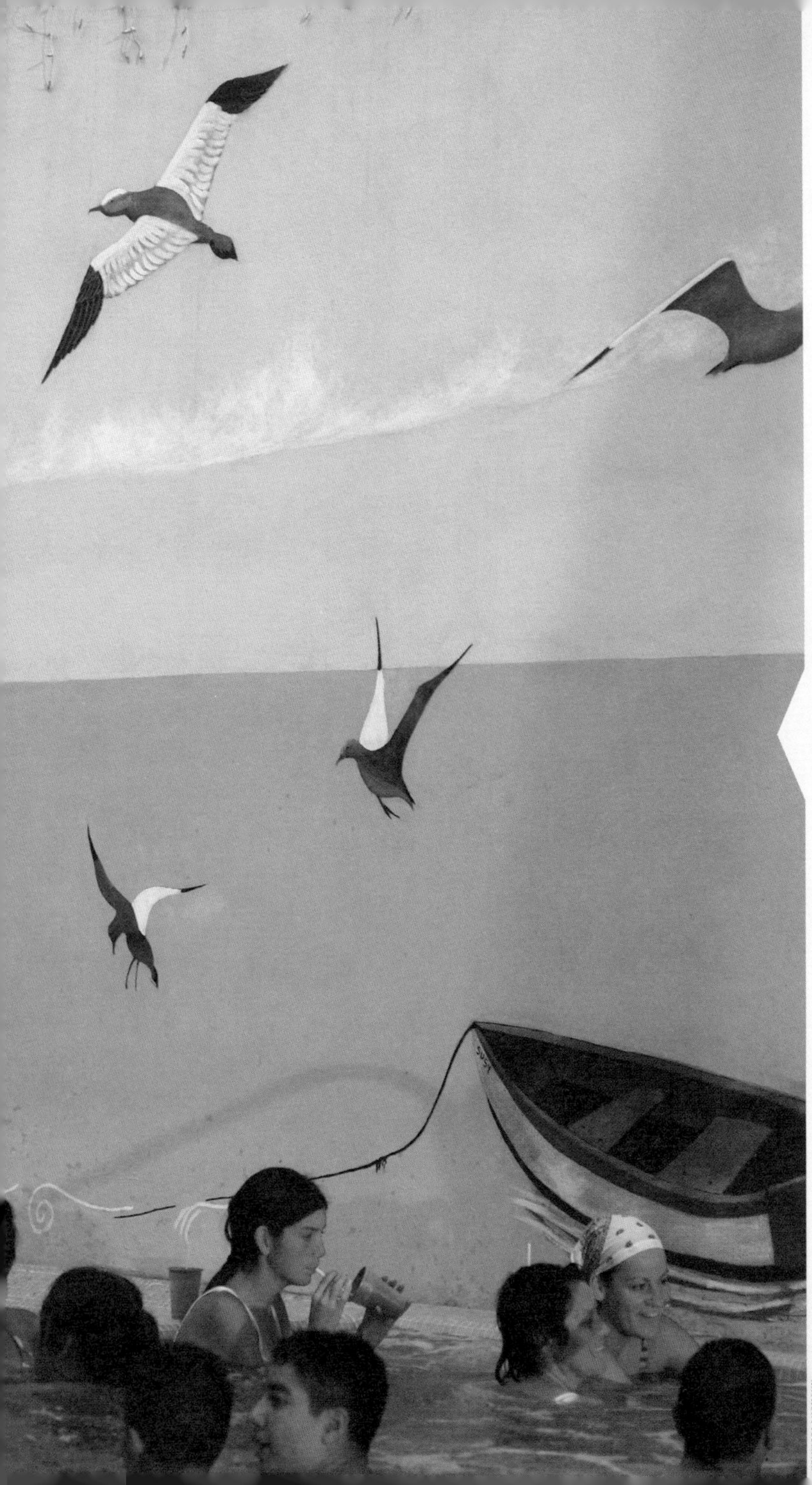

Puerto Vallarta, Mexico

ANTHONY PLUMMER

PARIS, FRANCE

Who the hell does Paris think it is? All that art, culture, history and romance. Yet this city remains so aloof. You don't want to fall for someone who doesn't care. So you try to act cool. The Eiffel Tower? It's not that big. The Louvre? It's too big. The hotel room? Too cramped. The streets? Too busy. That intimate prix fixe restaurant that you found where you had a small vineyard champagne and a dozen oysters that burst with the flavours of Brittany? Admit it, you're in love.

Maputo, Mozambique

ARIADNE VAN ZANDBERGEN

ROME, ITALY

Caput Mundi (Capital of the World), the Eternal City, the city to which all roads lead, Rome has been mesmerising visitors for more than 2500 years. An addictive mix of classical culture and baroque beauty, of angry traffic and relentless noise, it's an exhausting place. Unfortunately, you'll never see it all – there are simply too many churches, monuments, museums and galleries to take in. The trick is not to worry about it. Stroll the streets, have an ice cream, stop for a coffee – in short, do as the Romans do.

Auckland, New Zealand

BHUTAN

The Kingdom of Bhutan teeters between contemporary and medieval: monks transcribe ancient Buddhist texts into laptop computers, traditionally dressed archers use alloy-steel bows and arrows, and its farsighted leaders maintain Bhutan's pristine environment and unique culture. The king is supposed to have said, 'I am not as much concerned about the Gross National Product as I am about the Gross National Happiness'. Since Bhutan's doors opened in 1974, visitors have been mesmerised by spectacular Himalayan scenery, impressive architecture and hospitable people.

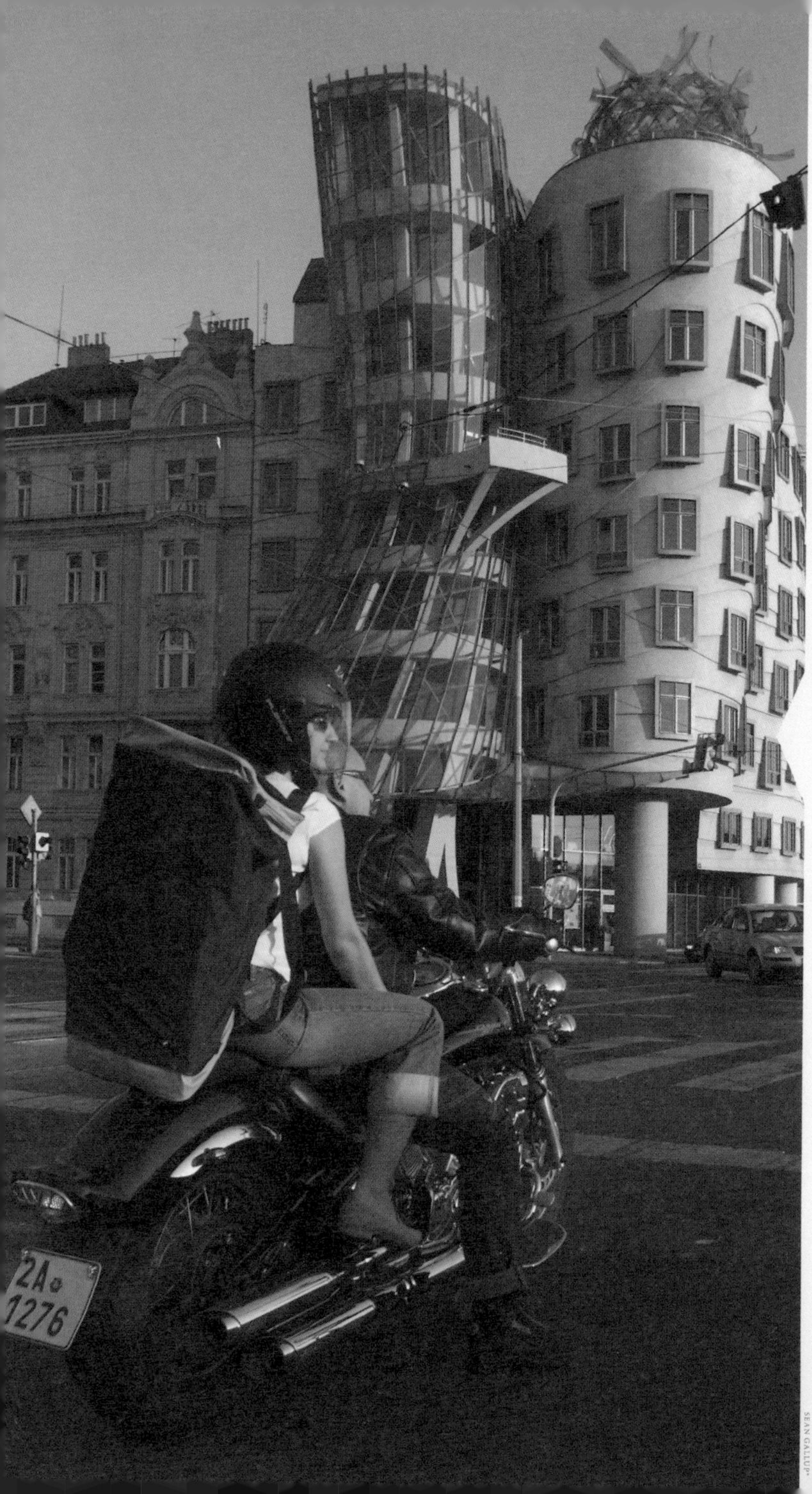

Prague, Czech Republic

SEAN GALLUP

PAPUA NEW GUINEA

Kundus and *garamut* drums beat out dizzying rhythms in the sweet sticky heat. The sound of insects rings in the air, and frogs and geckos bark as night falls, silenced only by a sudden deluge of tropical rain. The vegetation surrounding you is on growth hormones – overproductive, superabundant greenery. This is PNG, the quintessential Melanesian experience, filled with great mountain ranges, mighty rivers and stunning beaches, and five million people living much the way they have for thousands of years. And, as Randy Newman says, 'they got surfin' too'.

St Petersburg, Russia

BILL LYONS

TANZANIA

In northern Tanzania, Mt Kilimanjaro's stately snow-capped summit hovers majestically over the horizon, hundreds of flamingos stand sentinel in the salt pans on the floor of Ngorongoro Crater, and the hoof beats of thousands of wildebeest echo over the Serengeti plains. This is the Africa of legend, the quintessential snapshot of the continent, where hot, dusty afternoons end abruptly in glorious blazes of sunset, and velvet-black star-filled skies enfold the plains. It's a place where world-class safari lodges jostle for space with mud-thatch houses, where red-cloaked Maasai warriors follow centuries-old traditions, and where lively rural markets draw traders from miles around to haggle over everything from a head of cattle to a kilo of maize...

Bratislava, Slovakia

EGYPT

Egypt, the gift of the Nile, has captured the imagination since ancient times. Its awe-inspiring treasures – relics left by pharaohs, Greeks, Romans, Christians and Arabs alike – made it one of the world's first travel destinations. Around these age-old wonders, life forges on, as always at a crossroads between East and West, ancient and modern. And through everything, the majestic river flows, Egypt's lifeblood today as it has been since the dawn of history.

Bern, Switzerland

GLENN BEANLAND

BOSNIA-HERCEGOVINA

Sandwiched between Croatia and Serbia, the small mountainous country of Bosnia-Hercegovina has been a zone of contention since Occident and Orient first began arm-wrestling for it nearly two millennia ago. It's been through Christian, Muslim and Orthodox hands, and for a while its people seemed to enjoy their multicultural milieu. Then came the devastating war of the 1990s. Despite the destruction of much of its heritage, progress since then has been substantial and Bosnia-Hercegovina shows proud resilience through its scars. Gorgeous Sarajevo is waking back to life and driving through the craggy, dramatic countryside is unforgettable.

ANGKOR, CAMBODIA

Ta Prohm, one of the most intriguing ruins at Angkor, has been left to be swallowed by the jungle, and looks very much the way most of the monuments appeared when European explorers first stumbled upon them. The temple is cloaked in dappled shadow, its crumbling towers and walls locked in the slow muscular embrace of vast root systems. If Angkor Wat, the Bayon and other temples are testimony to the genius of the ancient Khmers, Ta Prohm reminds us equally of the awesome fecundity and power of the jungle. There is a poetic cycle to this venerable ruin, with humans first conquering nature to rapidly create, and nature once again conquering humans to slowly destroy.

NEW YORK CITY, USA

When Atlanta Braves pitcher John Rocker denounced New York City as a hateful place full of foreigners, young upstarts and queer people, New Yorkers couldn't have been more confused: What was bad about any of that? The city's diversity is what most folks find beautiful, mesmerising and addictive. Plus, NYC is a place where you'll find yourself witnessing miracles several times a day – like when the angry-looking frat boy drops a dollar into a street busker's basket, when flirty strangers exchange numbers on a subway, when buses run on time and new skyscrapers get built and you stumble into a hole-in-the-wall pub to find the most brilliant poetry reading you could ever imagine. It's brash, it's sexy, it's brilliant.

Washington, DC, USA

JEFF HUTCHENS

world map

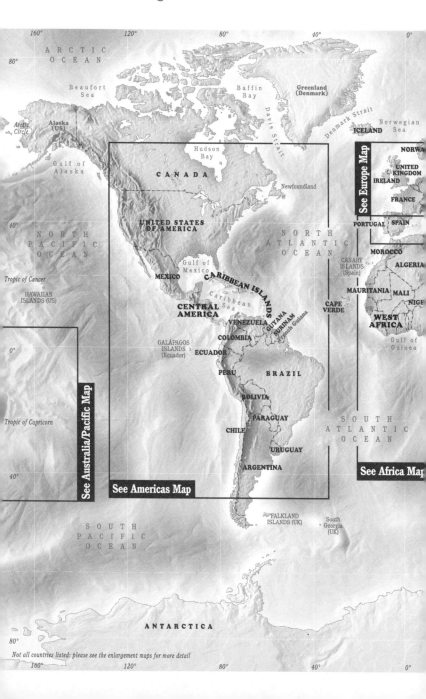

ARCTIC OCEAN

80°

Beaufort Sea

Arctic Circle

Alaska (US)

Gulf of Alaska

40°

NORTH PACIFIC OCEAN

Tropic of Cancer

HAWAIIAN ISLANDS (US)

0°

See Australia/Pacific Map

Tropic of Capricorn

40°

80°

SOUTH PACIFIC OCEAN

See Americas Map

Baffin Bay

Greenland (Denmark)

Denmark Strait

Norwegian Sea

ICELAND

Davis Strait

See Europe Map

NORWAY

UNITED KINGDOM

IRELAND

FRANCE

PORTUGAL   SPAIN

Hudson Bay

CANADA

Newfoundland

UNITED STATES OF AMERICA

NORTH ATLANTIC OCEAN

MOROCCO

ALGERIA

Gulf of Mexico

MEXICO

CARIBBEAN ISLANDS

Caribbean Sea

CENTRAL AMERICA

VENEZUELA   GUYANA

SURINAM

French Guiana

COLOMBIA

GALÁPAGOS ISLANDS (Ecuador)

ECUADOR

PERU

BRAZIL

BOLIVIA

PARAGUAY

CHILE

URUGUAY

ARGENTINA

CANARY ISLANDS (Spain)

MAURITANIA   MALI

NIGER

CAPE VERDE

WEST AFRICA

Gulf of Guinea

SOUTH ATLANTIC OCEAN

See Africa Map

FALKLAND ISLANDS (UK)

South Georgia (UK)

ANTARCTICA

Not all countries listed: please see the enlargement maps for more detail

160°   120°   80°   40°   0°

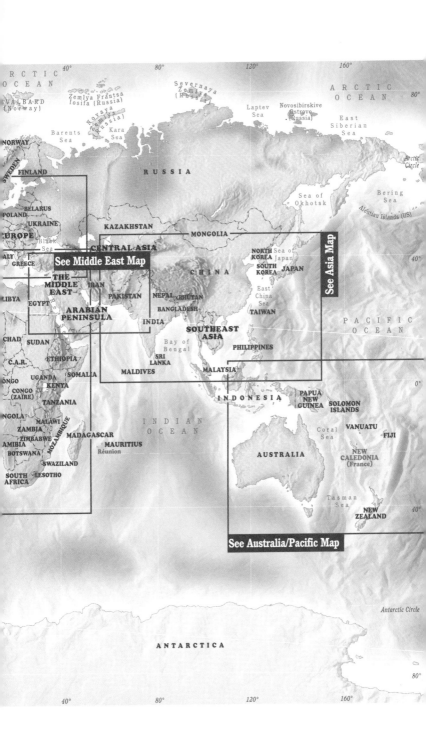

Aral
Sea

KAZAKHSTAN

TURKMENISTAN
UZBEKISTAN

MONGOLIA

Tashkent
Bishkek
KYRGYZSTAN

Samarkand

Dushanbe
TAJIKISTAN

Ürümqi

Dalandzadagad
Sainshand

Kerman

IRAN

Herat
AFGHANISTAN
Kabul
Kashgar

Hohhot
Beijing
Changchun
Haerbin

Jilin

Muscat

Kandahar
Islamabad

Shenyáng
Vladivostok

OMAN

Quetta

Lahore
Jammu &
Kashmir
(disputed)

Yinchuan
Shijiazhuang
Tiánjin

NORTH
KOREA
Pyongyang

Sapporo

Karachi
PAKISTAN
Sukkur

Jodhpur
Jaipur
Delhi
Agra

Tibet

Xining
Lánzhou
Táiyuán

Seoul
SOUTH
KOREA

JAPAN

Arabian
Sea
Hyderabad

Ahmedabad
Varanasi
NEPAL
Kathmandu
BHUTAN
Thimphu

Zhèngzhou
Xi'an

Jínán
Yellow
Sea
Kobe Osaka

Kyoto

Muscat

Hyderabad

INDIA
Mumbai
(Bombay)
Panaji
(Panjim)

Surat

Lhasa

CHINA

Héféi
Nánjing
Shànghai

Tokyo

Bangalore

Hyderabad
Vijayawada
Kolkata
(Calcutta)
Dhaka
BANGLADESH
Mandalay

Chéngdu

Wuhan
Hángzhou

East
China Sea

Colombo
SRI
LANKA

Madras
Bay
of
Bengal

Cuttack

MYANMAR
(BURMA)

Kunming
Guìyáng
Chángsha

Nánchang
Fúzhou

MALDIVES

INDIAN OCEAN

Bijayawada

Yangon
Chiang
Mai

Nánníng
Guangzhou
TAIWAN

Taipei

Phuket

THAILAND

Bangkok

LAOS
Vientiane

Hanoi
Haikou

VIETNAM

Macau Hong Kong

Georgetown
Kuala Lumpur
MALAYSIA
Singapore SINGAPORE

Penh
CAMBODIA
Phnom

Hồ Chí Minh
City
(Saigon)

South
China
Sea

PHILIPPINES
Manila

Philippine Sea

Davao

PACIFIC
OCEAN

BRUNEI
Bandar
Seri Begawan

INDONESIA

Celebes
Sea

PALAU

GUAM

Northern
Mariana
Islands
(US)

websites

Travel Information

www.lonelyplanet.com

Lonely Planet
destinations, guidebook upgrades, Thorn Tree,
links, world news, traveller's tales – it's all here

www.itisnet.com

Internet Travel Info Service
destination information and advice

www.fco.gov.uk

British Foreign & Commonwealth Office
travel advice written for Brits, but useful to all

http://travel.state.gov/travel

US Department of State
has a Travel Warnings section, with mildly
paranoid briefs about world trouble spots

Places to Stay

www.hotelguide.com

The Hotel Guide
international hotels bookable online

www.hostels.com

Internet Guide to Hostelling
worldwide hostels network

Activities

www.gorp.com

Great Outdoor Recreation Page
get into the great outdoors, from rafting to
wildlife refuges

World Events Calendar

www.festpass.com

World Events Calendar
world festivals sourced by area, keyword and date

Communications

www.netcafes.com

Internet café guide
search over 165 countries for your nearest
cyberccino

Local Times Around the World

www.timeanddate.com
/worldclock

Local Times Around the World
is it too late to ring home? Find out here

www.lonelyplanet.ekit.com

ekit
low-cost calls, email, voice messaging and
24-hour multilingual customer service

Health

www.who.int

World Health Organization
scare yourself with the world's diseases and
epidemics

www.tmvc.com.au

TMVC Healthy Travel
world vaccination chart and loads of travel
health info

Media

http://news.bbc.co.uk

BBC News
quality world news, with a quality British accent

www.cnn.com

CNN
American world news service

Photography

www.photo.net

Photo.net
advice on taking ace snaps

Money

www.mastercard.com/atm

MasterCard & Cirrus
fast ATM cash almost anywhere in the world

www.visa.com/pd/atm/main.html

Visa & Plus
fast ATM cash almost anywhere in the world

www.oanda.com/converter/classic

Oanda currency converter
the niftiest currency converter on the web

Visas

www3.travel.com.au

Travel.com.au's visa requirements
see Visas in the Travel Tools section to apply for visas hassle-free

Weather

www.rainorshine.com

Rain or Shine
five-day forecasts for 800 cities

Getting There & Away

www.travelocity.com

Travelocity
US-based online budget flight booker

www.statravel.com

STA Travel
international student flights booking agents

www.istc.org

International Student Travel Confederation
discounts and membership for students

http://upl.codeq.info

The Universal Packing List
gives tips on how to pack and what to leave behind

Entertainment

www.bored.com

Bored.com
from scamming your way into lawschool to translating websites into cockney – it's all here

www.snopes.com

Urban Legends Reference Pages
the urban legends homepage to spoil all those juicy rumours

conversions

Women's Clothing

Dresses, coats, suits, jumpers/sweaters

Australia/NZ	8	10	12	14	16	18	20
Europe	36	38	40	42	44	46	48
Japan	5	7	9	11	13	15	17
UK	8	10	12	14	16	18	20
USA	6	8	10	12	14	16	18

Shoes

Australia/NZ	5	5½	6	6½	7	7½	8	8½	9	9½	10
Europe	35	36	36	37	37	38	38	39	39	40	40
France only	35	35	36	37	38	38	39	39	40	41	42
Japan	22	22½	23	23½	24	24½	25	25½	26	26½	27
UK	3½	4	4½	5	5½	6	6½	7	7½	8	8½
USA	5	5½	6	6½	7	7½	8	8½	9	9½	10

Men's Clothing

Suits, jackets, jumpers/sweaters

Australia/NZ	88	92	96	100	104	108	112	116	120
Europe	44	46	48	50	52	54	56	58	60
Japan	S				M				L
UK	34	35	36	37	38	39	40	41	42
USA	34	35	36	37	38	39	40	41	42

Shirts (collar sizes)

Australia/NZ	37	38	39	40	41	42	43	44	45
Europe	37	38	39	40	41	42	43	44	45
Japan	37	38	39	40	41	42	43	44	45
UK	14½	15	15½	16	16½	17	17½	18	18½
USA	14½	15	15½	16	16½	17	17½	18	18½

Shoes

Australia/NZ	6	7	8	9	10	11	12
Europe	40	41	42	43	44½	46	47
Japan	25	26	27	27½	28	29	30
UK	6	7	8	9	10	11	12
USA	6½	7½	8½	9½	10½	11½	12½

Temperature

to convert	multiply by	and add
°C to °F	1.8	32

to convert	subtract	and divide by
°F to °C	32	1.8

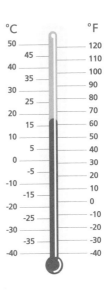

Volume

to convert	to	multiply by
imperial gallons	litres	4.55
litres	imperial gallons	0.22
US gallons	litres	3.79
litres	US gallons	0.26

also
5 imperial gallons equal just over 6 US gallons, a litre is slightly more than a US quart, slightly less than a British quart

Length, Distance & Area

to convert	to	multiply by
inches	centimetres	2.54
centimetres	inches	0.39
feet	metres	0.30
metres	feet	3.28
yards	metres	0.91
metres	yards	1.09
miles	kilometres	1.61
kilometres	miles	0.62
acres	hectares	0.40
hectares	acres	2.47

Weight

to convert	to	multiply by
ounces	grams	28.35
grams	ounces	0.035
pounds	kilograms	0.45
kilograms	pounds	2.21
British tons	kilograms	1016
US tons	kilograms	907

also
a British ton is 2240lbs
a US ton is 2000lbs
a metric tonne is 1000kg

international dialling codes

COUNTRY **CODE** DIAL OUT

AFGHANISTAN **93** 00
ALBANIA **355** 00
ALGERIA **213** 00
ANDORRA **376** 00
ANGOLA **244** 00
ANGUILLA **1+264** 011
ANTIGUA & BARBUDA **1+268** 011
ARGENTINA **54** 00
ARMENIA **374** 00
ARUBA **297** 00
ASCENSION ISLAND **247** 01
AUSTRALIA **61** 0011
AUSTRIA **43** 00
AZERBAIJAN **994** 8-10
BAHAMAS **1+242** 011
BAHRAIN **973** 0
BANGLADESH **880** 00
BARBADOS **1+246** 011
BELARUS **375** 8-10
BELGIUM **32** 00
BELIZE **501** 00
BENIN **229** 00
BERMUDA **1+441** 011
BHUTAN **975** 00
BOLIVIA **591** 00
BOSNIA-HERCEGOVINA · **387** 00
BOTSWANA **267** 00
BRAZIL **55** 00
BRUNEI DARUSSALAM **673** 00
BULGARIA **359** 00
BURKINA FASO **226** 00
BURUNDI **257** 90
CAMBODIA **855** 00
CAMEROON **237** 00
CANADA **1** 011
CAPE VERDE **238** 0
CAYMAN ISLANDS **1+345** 011
CENTRAL AFRICAN REPUBLIC **236** 19
CHAD **235** 15
CHILE **56** 00
CHINA **86** 00
COLOMBIA **57** 009
COMOROS **269** 10
CONGO **242** 00
COOK ISLANDS **682** 00
COSTA RICA **506** 00
CÔTE D'IVOIRE **225** 00
CROATIA **385** 00
CUBA **53** 119
CYPRUS **357** 00
CYPRUS (TURK OCCUPIED) **90+392** 00
CZECH REPUBLIC **420** 00
DENMARK **45** 00
DIEGO GARCIA **246** 00
DJIBOUTI **253** 00
DOMINICA ISLAND **1+767** 011
DOMINICAN REPUBLIC **1+767** 011
ECUADOR **593** 00
EGYPT **20** 00
EL SALVADOR **503** 00
EQUATORIAL GUINEA **240** 00
ERITREA **291** 00
ESTONIA **372** 8-00
ETHIOPIA **251** 00
FALKLAND ISLANDS **500** 0
FAROE ISLANDS **298** 009
FIJI **679** 05
FINLAND **358** 00
FORMER YUGOSLAV REPUBLIC OF
   MACEDONIA **389** 00
FRANCE **33** 00
FRENCH GUIANA **594** 00
FRENCH POLYNESIA **689** 00
GABON **241** 00

GAMBIA (THE) **220** 00
GEORGIA **995** 8-10
GERMANY **49** 00
GHANA **233** 00
GIBRALTAR **350** 00
GREECE **30** 00
GREENLAND **299** 009
GRENADA **1+473** 011
GUADELOUPE **590** 00
GUAM **1+671** 011
GUATEMALA **502** 00
GUINEA **224** 00
GUINEA-BISSAU **245** 00
GUYANA **592** 001
HAITI **509** 00
HONDURAS **504** 00
HONG KONG **852** 001
HUNGARY **36** 00
ICELAND **354** 00
INDIA **91** 00
INDONESIA **62** 001 or 008
IRAN **98** 00
IRAQ **964** 00
IRELAND (NORTH) **44** 00
IRELAND (REP) **353** 00
ISRAEL **972** 00
ITALY **39** 00
JAMAICA **1+876** 011
JAPAN **81** 001
JORDAN **962** 00
KAZAKHSTAN **7** 8-10
KENYA **254** 000
KIRIBATI **686** 00
KOREA (NORTH) **850** 00
KOREA (SOUTH) **82** 001.
LAOS **856** 14
LATVIA **371** 00
LEBANON **961** 00
LESOTHO **266** 00
LIBERIA **231** 00
LIBYA **218** 00
LIECHTENSTEIN **423** 00
LITHUANIA **370** 8-10
LUXEMBOURG **352** 00
MADAGASCAR **261** 00
MALAWI **265** 101
MALAYSIA **60** 00
MALDIVES **960** 00
MALI **223** 00
MALTA **356** 00
MARSHALL ISLANDS **692** 011
MARTINIQUE **596** 00
MAURITANIA **222** 00
MAURITIUS **230** 00
MAYOTTE **269** 10
MEXICO **52** 00
MICRONESIA **691** 011
MOLDOVA **373** 8-10
MONACO **377** 00
MONGOLIA **976** 00
MONTSERRAT **1+664** 011
MOROCCO **212** 00
MOZAMBIQUE **258** 00
MYANMAR (BURMA) **95** 0
NAMIBIA **264** 09
NAURU **674** 00
NEPAL **977** 00
NETHERLANDS **31** 00
NETHERLANDS ANTILLES **599** 00
NEW CALEDONIA **687** 00
NEW ZEALAND **64** 00
NICARAGUA **505** 00
NIGER **227** 00
NIGERIA **234** 009
NORWAY **47** 00

OMAN **968** 00
PAKISTAN **92** 00
PALAU **680** 011
PANAMA **507** 0
PAPUA NEW GUINEA **675** 05
PARAGUAY **595** 00
PERU **51** 00
PHILIPPINES **63** 00
POLAND **48** 00
PORTUGAL **351** 00
PUERTO RICO **1+787** 011
QATAR **974** 0
REUNION **262** 00
ROMANIA **40** 00
RUSSIA **7** 8-10
RWANDA **250** 00
ST HELENA **290** 01
ST KITTS & NEVIS **1+869** 011
ST LUCIA **1+758** 011
ST PIERRE & MIQUELON **508** 00
ST VINCENT & THE
   GRENADINES **1+809** 011
SAMOA (AMERICAN) **684** 00
SÃO TOMÉ & PRÍNCIPE **239** 00
SAUDI ARABIA **966** 00
SENEGAL **221** 00
SERBIA & MONTENEGRO **381** 99
SEYCHELLES **248** 00
SIERRA LEONE **232** 00
SINGAPORE **65** 001
SLOVAK REPUBLIC **421** 00
SLOVENIA **386** 00
SOLOMON ISLANDS **677** 00
SOMALIA **252** 19
SOUTH AFRICA **27** 09
SPAIN **34** 00
SRI LANKA **94** 00
SUDAN **249** 00
SURINAME **597** 00
SWAZILAND **268** 00
SWEDEN **46** 00
SWITZERLAND **41** 00
SYRIA **963** 00
TAIWAN **886** 002
TAJIKISTAN **992** 8-10
TANZANIA **255** 000
THAILAND **66** 001
TOGO **228** 00
TONGA **676** 00
TRINIDAD & TOBAGO **1+868** 011
TUNISIA **216** 00
TURKEY **90** 00
TURKMENISTAN **993** 8-10
TURKS & CAICOS ISLANDS **1+649** 01
TUVALU **688** 00
UGANDA **256** 000
UK **44** 00
UKRAINE **380** 8-10
UNITED ARAB EMIRATES **971** 00
URUGUAY **598** 00
USA **1** 011
UZBEKISTAN **998** 8-10
VANUATU **678** 00
VATICAN CITY **39** 00
VENEZUELA **58** 00
VIETNAM **84** 00
VIRGIN ISLANDS (UK) **1+809496** 01
VIRGIN ISLANDS (USA) **1+340** 011
WALLIS & FUTUNA ISLANDS **681** 19
YEMEN **967** 00
YUGOSLAVIA **381** 99
ZAMBIA **260** 00
ZIMBABWE **263** 00

world languages

This isn't how I normally meet people.
Dlya minya eta vis'ma niabihchnih sposap znakomstva (Russian)

Could you put some sunscreen on my back, please?
Možeš li mi staviti kremu protiv sunca na le a, molim? (Croatian)

What's your favourite team?
Qual é la tua squadra preferita? (Italian)

Where's an ice-cream café?
Gdye yest' kafeh-marozhenaye? (Russian)

Where can I get tickets to the bullfight?
¿Dónde se compran las entradas para los toros? (Spanish)

This is a different dish of cabbage!
Ez más káposzta! (Hungarian)

Do you come here often?
Vieni Spesso qua? (Italian)

When cows fly!
Kun lehmät lentää! (Finnish)

Get lost!
Goni se! (Croatian)

Where are we?
¿Lumi kasem long wea? (Solomon Islands Pijin)

Do you have a smoke sauna?
Onko teillä savusauna? (Finnish)

Do you have something cheaper?
Mii thùuk-kwàa níi mãi (Thai)

I'm not good at singing (karaoke).
Watashi wa uta ga jozu ja arimasen (Japanese)

Would you like a drink?
¿Te apetece una copa? (Spanish)

Lets have a drink!
Buvons un coup! (French)

Eat, my son/daughter. Let it rip!
Jedi sinko/kćeri, samo udri! (Croatian)

May it contribute to your health!
Afiyet olsun! (Turkish, said before eating)

I love animals so I don't eat them.
Ya lyublyu zhihvotnihkh paetamu ya nye yem ikh. (Russian)

I want to go for Yum Cha.
Ngoh seung hui yum cha. (Cantonese)

I would like to see an acrobatic troupe.
Wo xian kan zajituan. (Mandarin Chinese)

I would like to have a rest.
Maref ëfellëgallo. (Ethiopian Amharic)

calendars

2005

JANUARY

S	M	T	W	T	F	S
30	31					1
2	3	4	5	6	7	8
9	10	11	12	13	14	15
16	17	18	19	20	21	22
23	24	25	26	27	28	29

FEBRUARY

S	M	T	W	T	F	S
		1	2	3	4	5
6	7	8	9	10	11	12
13	14	15	16	17	18	19
20	21	22	23	24	25	26
27	28					

MARCH

S	M	T	W	T	F	S
		1	2	3	4	5
6	7	8	9	10	11	12
13	14	15	16	17	18	19
20	21	22	23	24	25	26
27	28	29	30	31		

APRIL

S	M	T	W	T	F	S
					1	2
3	4	5	6	7	8	9
10	11	12	13	14	15	16
17	18	19	20	21	22	23
24	25	26	27	28	29	30

MAY

S	M	T	W	T	F	S
1	2	3	4	5	6	7
8	9	10	11	12	13	14
15	16	17	18	19	20	21
22	23	24	25	26	27	28
29	30	31				

JUNE

S	M	T	W	T	F	S
			1	2	3	4
5	6	7	8	9	10	11
12	13	14	15	16	17	18
19	20	21	22	23	24	25
26	27	28	29	30		

JULY

S	M	T	W	T	F	S
31					1	2
3	4	5	6	7	8	9
10	11	12	13	14	15	16
17	18	19	20	21	22	23
24	25	26	27	28	29	30

AUGUST

S	M	T	W	T	F	S
	1	2	3	4	5	6
7	8	9	10	11	12	13
14	15	16	17	18	19	20
21	22	23	24	25	26	27
28	29	30	31			

SEPTEMBER

S	M	T	W	T	F	S
				1	2	3
4	5	6	7	8	9	10
11	12	13	14	15	16	17
18	19	20	21	22	23	24
25	26	27	28	29	30	

OCTOBER

S	M	T	W	T	F	S
30	31					1
2	3	4	5	6	7	8
9	10	11	12	13	14	15
16	17	18	19	20	21	22
23	24	25	26	27	28	29

NOVEMBER

S	M	T	W	T	F	S
		1	2	3	4	5
6	7	8	9	10	11	12
13	14	15	16	17	18	19
20	21	22	23	24	25	26
27	28	29	30			

DECEMBER

S	M	T	W	T	F	S
				1	2	3
4	5	6	7	8	9	10
11	12	13	14	15	16	17
18	19	20	21	22	23	24
25	26	27	28	29	30	31

2006

JANUARY

S	M	T	W	T	F	S
1	2	3	4	5	6	7
8	9	10	11	12	13	14
15	16	17	18	19	20	21
22	23	24	25	26	27	28
29	30	31				

FEBRUARY

S	M	T	W	T	F	S
			1	2	3	4
5	6	7	8	9	10	11
12	13	14	15	16	17	18
19	20	21	22	23	24	25
26	27	28				

MARCH

S	M	T	W	T	F	S
			1	2	3	4
5	6	7	8	9	10	11
12	13	14	15	16	17	18
19	20	21	22	23	24	25
26	27	28	29	30	31	

APRIL

S	M	T	W	T	F	S
30						1
2	3	4	5	6	7	8
9	10	11	12	13	14	15
16	17	18	19	20	21	22
23	24	25	26	27	28	29

MAY

S	M	T	W	T	F	S
	1	2	3	4	5	6
7	8	9	10	11	12	13
14	15	16	17	18	19	20
21	22	23	24	25	26	27
28	29	30	31			

JUNE

S	M	T	W	T	F	S
				1	2	3
4	5	6	7	8	9	10
11	12	13	14	15	16	17
18	19	20	21	22	23	24
25	26	27	28	29	30	

JULY

S	M	T	W	T	F	S
30	31					1
2	3	4	5	6	7	8
9	10	11	12	13	14	15
16	17	18	19	20	21	22
23	24	25	26	27	28	29

AUGUST

S	M	T	W	T	F	S
		1	2	3	4	5
6	7	8	9	10	11	12
13	14	15	16	17	18	19
20	21	22	23	24	25	26
27	28	29	30	31		

SEPTEMBER

S	M	T	W	T	F	S
					1	2
3	4	5	6	7	8	9
10	11	12	13	14	15	16
17	18	19	20	21	22	23
24	25	26	27	28	29	30

OCTOBER

S	M	T	W	T	F	S
1	2	3	4	5	6	7
8	9	10	11	12	13	14
15	16	17	18	19	20	21
22	23	24	25	26	27	28
29	30	31				

NOVEMBER

S	M	T	W	T	F	S
			1	2	3	4
5	6	7	8	9	10	11
12	13	14	15	16	17	18
19	20	21	22	23	24	25
26	27	28	29	30		

DECEMBER

S	M	T	W	T	F	S
31					1	2
3	4	5	6	7	8	9
10	11	12	13	14	15	16
17	18	19	20	21	22	23
24	25	26	27	28	29	30

2007

JANUARY
S	M	T	W	T	F	S
	1	2	3	4	5	6
7	8	9	10	11	12	13
14	15	16	17	18	19	20
21	22	23	24	25	26	27
28	29	30	31			

FEBRUARY
S	M	T	W	T	F	S
				1	2	3
4	5	6	7	8	9	10
11	12	13	14	15	16	17
18	19	20	21	22	23	24
25	26	27	28			

MARCH
S	M	T	W	T	F	S
				1	2	3
4	5	6	7	8	9	10
11	12	13	14	15	16	17
18	19	20	21	22	23	24
25	26	27	28	29	30	31

APRIL
S	M	T	W	T	F	S
1	2	3	4	5	6	7
8	9	10	11	12	13	14
15	16	17	18	19	20	21
22	23	24	25	26	27	28
29	30					

MAY
S	M	T	W	T	F	S
		1	2	3	4	5
6	7	8	9	10	11	12
13	14	15	16	17	18	19
20	21	22	23	24	25	26
27	28	29	30	31		

JUNE
S	M	T	W	T	F	S
					1	2
3	4	5	6	7	8	9
10	11	12	13	14	15	16
17	18	19	20	21	22	23
24	25	26	27	28	29	30

JULY
S	M	T	W	T	F	S
1	2	3	4	5	6	7
8	9	10	11	12	13	14
15	16	17	18	19	20	21
22	23	24	25	26	27	28
29	30	31				

AUGUST
S	M	T	W	T	F	S
			1	2	3	4
5	6	7	8	9	10	11
12	13	14	15	16	17	18
19	20	21	22	23	24	25
26	27	28	29	30	31	

SEPTEMBER
S	M	T	W	T	F	S
30						1
2	3	4	5	6	7	8
9	10	11	12	13	14	15
16	17	18	19	20	21	22
23	24	25	26	27	28	29

OCTOBER
S	M	T	W	T	F	S
	1	2	3	4	5	6
7	8	9	10	11	12	13
14	15	16	17	18	19	20
21	22	23	24	25	26	27
28	29	30	31			

NOVEMBER
S	M	T	W	T	F	S
				1	2	3
4	5	6	7	8	9	10
11	12	13	14	15	16	17
18	19	20	21	22	23	24
25	26	27	28	29	30	

DECEMBER
S	M	T	W	T	F	S
30	31					1
2	3	4	5	6	7	8
9	10	11	12	13	14	15
16	17	18	19	20	21	22
23	24	25	26	27	28	29

2008

JANUARY
S	M	T	W	T	F	S
		1	2	3	4	5
6	7	8	9	10	11	12
13	14	15	16	17	18	19
20	21	22	23	24	25	26
27	28	29	30	31		

FEBRUARY
S	M	T	W	T	F	S
					1	2
3	4	5	6	7	8	9
10	11	12	13	14	15	16
17	18	19	20	21	22	23
24	25	26	27	28	29	

MARCH
S	M	T	W	T	F	S
30	31					1
2	3	4	5	6	7	8
9	10	11	12	13	14	15
16	17	18	19	20	21	22
23	24	25	26	27	28	29

APRIL
S	M	T	W	T	F	S
		1	2	3	4	5
6	7	8	9	10	11	12
13	14	15	16	17	18	19
20	21	22	23	24	25	26
27	28	29	30			

MAY
S	M	T	W	T	F	S
				1	2	3
4	5	6	7	8	9	10
11	12	13	14	15	16	17
18	19	20	21	22	23	24
25	26	27	28	29	30	31

JUNE
S	M	T	W	T	F	S
1	2	3	4	5	6	7
8	9	10	11	12	13	14
15	16	17	18	19	20	21
22	23	24	25	26	27	28
29	30					

JULY
S	M	T	W	T	F	S
		1	2	3	4	5
6	7	8	9	10	11	12
13	14	15	16	17	18	19
20	21	22	23	24	25	26
27	28	29	30	31		

AUGUST
S	M	T	W	T	F	S
31					1	2
3	4	5	6	7	8	9
10	11	12	13	14	15	16
17	18	19	20	21	22	23
24	25	26	27	28	29	30

SEPTEMBER
S	M	T	W	T	F	S
	1	2	3	4	5	6
7	8	9	10	11	12	13
14	15	16	17	18	19	20
21	22	23	24	25	26	27
28	29	30				

OCTOBER
S	M	T	W	T	F	S
			1	2	3	4
5	6	7	8	9	10	11
12	13	14	15	16	17	18
19	20	21	22	23	24	25
26	27	28	29	30	31	

NOVEMBER
S	M	T	W	T	F	S
30						1
2	3	4	5	6	7	8
9	10	11	12	13	14	15
16	17	18	19	20	21	22
23	24	25	26	27	28	29

DECEMBER
S	M	T	W	T	F	S
	1	2	3	4	5	6
7	8	9	10	11	12	13
14	15	16	17	18	19	20
21	22	23	24	25	26	27
28	29	30	31			

the lonely planet story

Lonely Planet published its first book in 1973 in response to the numerous 'How did you do it?' questions Maureen and Tony Wheeler were asked after driving, busing, hitching, sailing and railing their way from England to Australia.

Written at a kitchen table and hand-collated, trimmed and stapled, *Across Asia on the Cheap* became an instant local bestseller, inspiring thoughts of another book.

Eighteen months in Southeast Asia resulted in the Wheelers' second guide, *South-East Asia on a shoestring*, which they put together in a backstreet Chinese hotel in Singapore in 1975. The 'yellow bible', as it quickly became known to backpackers around the world, soon became the guide to the region. It has sold well over half a million copies and is now in its 10th edition, still retaining its familiar yellow cover.

Today there are almost 500 titles, including travel guides, walking guides, phrasebooks, a travel literature series, travel reference titles and more. The company is the largest independent travel publisher in the world.

The emphasis continues to be on travel for independent travellers. Tony and Maureen still travel for several months each year and play an active part in the writing, updating and quality control of Lonely Planet's guides.

They have been joined by a team of authors around the world and staff at our offices in Melbourne (Australia), Oakland (USA) and London (UK). Travellers themselves also make a valuable contribution to the guides through the feedback we receive in thousands of letters each year and on our website.

Lonely Planet strongly believes that travellers can make a positive contribution to the countries they visit, both through their appreciation of the countries' culture, wildlife and natural features, and through the money they spend. In addition, the company makes a direct contribution to the countries and regions it covers. Since 1986 a percentage of the income from each book has been donated to ventures such as famine relief in Africa; aid projects in India; agricultural projects in Central America; Greenpeace's efforts to halt French nuclear testing in the Pacific; and Amnesty International.

For news, views and updates, see

www.lonelyplanet.com